GW01271915

Receptacle of Dreams

Selected Poems – Volume VI

Mary Cochrane

For Those Who Loved Me

"If I don't see you no more in this world, I'll meet you in the next one and don't be late."

Jimi Hendrix (1968)

CONTENTS

SHORT STORIES AND FACTUAL ACCOUNTS

Eyes That Hold All Secrets

Don't you feel it?
You and I are soulmates,
Riding on a higher plane.
I prayed for a love
That would surpass everything.

Now I float in a world
Of lilies and sweet things,
And the Moonlight Sonata
Invades my dreams.

Champagne days
And deep conversation,
Distract me from the thought
Of obliteration.

And there you are,
At the forefront of my mind;
Depicting the otherworldly
In a breathtaking form.

'Wake up!' the new voice calls,
And ushers me past the dawn
To the pinnacle of the day:
Another glimpse of those eyes
That hold all secrets.

[20.10.19 – to Gerry]

Concept of Utopia

It's funny how the universe
Can be contained in a person:
One unit which represents
A concept of Utopia.

It's sobering to witness
A lifespan in its final stage;
Trundling along and making
The most of limiting days.

It's the realms beyond the physical
That threaten the state of play,
With promises that cannot translate
Into this reality.

[20.10.19 – To Gerry]

Open To Love

Sometimes real life plays out in a manner
More captivating and unexpected
Than the imagination could conceptualise.
Sometimes a most significant person appears
When life is coursing on a downward slope
And each day is a sad repetition of itself.

Sometimes all that is needed is an alignment
Of the correct time, place and people,
To uphold a destiny of miraculous proportions:
All initiated by a flash of eyes,
The warm tones of a Celtic voice,
And a recipient's heart open to love.

[01.11.19]

Forgive Me!

John,
Come and take me home.

Gerry,
Here we go again -
What might have been.

Mike,
I found some respite
In your loving care.

Now the darkness stretches
In torturous places
Without sunlight or human faces.

I can't go on
In the storm
Of this disease.

I know you will forgive me.

[22.11.19]

Enshrouded

Life is a funny thing;
Strange and wondrous and tormenting.
Sometimes it runs at full kilter,
Then it splutters and ebbs
And wearies the best of us.

It may be unwise to place
Too much reliance on the status quo
Or to maintain the breakneck
Or even the sedentary pace;
Better to expect the unexpected:

Where there is beauty, hold it
For as long as fate dictates;
Where there is pain and sorrow,
Endure it with great fortitude;
For who knows when the darkness
Will enshroud us one last time?

[04.12.19]

Gerry Jones

There is a thing called eternity
And you can stretch your soul across it;
Away from the horrors of the slums
And the coldness of medical atrocities.

There is a Celtic man who rides with me
To the highest spiritual planes;
Whose eyes can uplift in the moments
When the physicality wanes.

His name is Gerry Jones and I love him.
He lives close by, in Llangefni town.
I'll be buried where I can be near him
When they lay me down in the Welsh ground.

[05.01.20]

Receptacle of Dreams

Hostile, tempestuous, desolate,
Unfit for human habitation.
Apocalyptic, damaged, forsaken;
Environmental devastation.

Stranded on an island defaced
Beyond the general milieu,
Crawling to the surface to witness
An unstable, fragmentary view.

Hopeless world, ready for implosion,
Sky closing on a blackened sun.
Storms rising in a vacuum,
Lost and searching for everyone.

Body weak, internal screaming,
Waves of trauma, nothing as it seems.
Pallbearers carrying the corpse
To the receptacle of dreams.

[10.02.20]

Mirror Image

I love you, Gerry Jones -
I love everything about you:
Your wild, unstoppable nature;
Those eyes that will take me
To the end of the world with a smile;
And the vast humanity
Emanating from your presence.

I love your smile and the sensual
Play of wickedness on your lips;
The way you move at breakneck pace
As I cast my wistful gaze upon you.

I see you as a mirror image
Of everything I used to be.
Each day is heartened by the joy
Of you returning home to me.

[10.02.20]

His Presence

I see beyond the everyday
In the silence of my lonely room.
With subtle mutability,
His presence lingers in the gloom.

In the silence of my lonely room
His image haunts me, all serene.
His presence lingers in the gloom;
A spectre from a ceaseless dream.

His image haunts me, all serene,
In waves of immortality;
A spectre from a ceaseless dream,
Regaling songs of liberty.

In waves of immortality
He moves with unassuming grace.
Regaling songs of liberty,
He takes me to that sacred place.

He moves with unassuming grace,
With subtle mutability.
He takes me to the sacred place
I see beyond the everyday.

[15.02.20 – To John]

The Sway of the Nightingale's Song

In the sway of the nightingale's song
I will dance with the stars above,
And depart from my sweet Ynys Môn
When the world is abundant with love.

I will dance with the stars above
When your soul is attuned to my own.
When the world is abundant with love,
I'll be beckoning you back home.

As your soul is attuned to my own,
In a flourish of ecstasy,
I'll be beckoning you back home
To a sense of belonging with me.

In a flourish of ecstasy
We will run with our wraiths and our kin.
With a sense of belonging we'll be
Awakened to Heaven again.

We will run with our wraiths and our kin
And depart from my sweet Ynys Môn;
Awakened to Heaven again,
In the sway of the nightingale's song.

[03.03.20]

Trauma

Mouth open but screams unheard,
Tethered to a world of pain.
The leaves are turning
And I am yearning again.

Mother and John in the grave now,
Family history fading with time.
Last semblance of life existing
Merely in the context of rhyme.

But 'he' comes by, personifying
The perfect archetypal king;
In warrior mode and allocating
The deepest meaning to everything.

Then midnight steals away all sanity
And through the gaps the trauma grips.
The world asleep and oblivious
As the life blood slowly drips.

[09.03.20]
'He' is Gerry Jones

Wishing

I wish I had told him,
When I visited our home town of Glasgow,
That I waited at the window
Each and every morning
To watch him stride across the waste ground.

I wish I had told him
That the sun shone in his blue eyes
And that the earth could not spin
Without the grace of his presence.

I wish I had told him
That, in the event of his leaving,
He should take me with him,
Otherwise my heart would shatter and break.

I wish my world would not implode
In the absence of his beauty;
But all these wishes are in vain
And I want to be with him again.

[31.03.20 – To John]

Coronavirus versus Cancer

Global update - Coronavirus
Acute situation -
Over one million now dead,
Government-imposed self-isolation as a means
Of controlling the spread
And thereby reducing fatalities.

Dire humanistic and economic consequences,
And mental health concerns.
Unprecedented: Incomparable with war
Or anything known before.
NHS workers on the front line
And all the world waiting for a time
When it will stop.

Personal update - Cancer
Chronic situation -
Fourteen years of unrelenting illness;
Self-imposed isolation as a means
Of conserving minimal energy
And hiding unsociable symptomatology.

Dire humanistic consequences
And mental health impact.
Unprecedented:
Unmanageable, prolonged battle;
Nursing a body and mind
That should have expired long ago.
The sense of hopelessly waiting
And so deeply alone.

[04.04.20]

Desperate Land

It was too late by then -
The wind and rain
Had set upon her son's grave
And psychiatric services
Were knocking at her door.
She was metaphorically
Laid out on the floor,
Detached from all she had known before.

"I've lost myself," she constantly said
As the torturous voices
Rattled in her head,
Infiltrating every drawn-out day
And rendering sleep an impossibility.

"I've lost myself," she said
Until my heart bled,
But only now do I truly understand
The enormity of falling into
That desperate land.

[04.04.20]

Rapture

There is rapture in each new day
When you are standing by my side.
Your eyes, like diamonds, can convey
The essence of the rushing tide.

When you are standing by my side,
My shattered heart begins to soothe.
The essence of the rushing tide
Reflects your power as my muse.

My shattered heart begins to soothe
And fortune, like an ancient king,
Reflects your power as my muse
And your influence on everything.

And fortune, like an ancient king,
Reminds me that our love will last,
And your influence on everything
Cannot be broken or surpassed.

Reminds me that our love will last
And your eyes, like diamonds will convey
What can't be broken or surpassed.
There is rapture in each new day.

[28.04.20 – To Gerry]

The Lockdown Guest

Lockdown is of no consequence
In the prison of this body.
My perilous, illicit guest
Is the only one who saves me.

In the prison of this body
Is a silent desperation,
And only one can save me
From this state of desolation.

In a silent desperation
I contemplate unseemly things;
In a state of desolation
That mirrors unsafe happenings.

I contemplate unseemly things
In secretive activities
That mirror unsafe happenings
And unspeakable proclivities.

In secretive activities
My perilous, illicit guest
Has unspeakable proclivities.
Lockdown is of no consequence.

[27.06.20 – To Gerry]

All and Everything

I want you to read these works
And feel the intensity
That only kindred spirits do.
I want you to feel my presence
In the very depths of you.

There is no relevance
In how events unfold
Or words are uttered day-to-day.
A constant challenge will erode
The superficial parody:

It will manifest as a smile
Or a flicker of our eyes
When we read between the lines.
It will incur the dread
Of restlessness and sleepless nights.

Only when I inadvertently
Threaten to slip away from
Life's great melting-pot of joy and pain,
Will you reach beyond the boundary
And try to pull me back again.

I do not judge although I'm deemed
To be dallying with insanity.
I will give you all and everything
And love you for eternity.

[30.06.20]

Dark Tide

I love him endlessly
And I paint his image
In the landscape of my mind.
In all these gruelling years
I have never found
Solace of a better kind.

How often the sweetness
Is rendered bitter
By the black of the demon pain;
How swiftly the laughter
Is rendered hollow
When all my efforts are in vain.

I have trodden my life's path
With a grim companion
Who has, sadly, never left my side.
I am battle-worn
And willing to slip
Beneath the waves of his dark tide.

[02.07.20]

Seed of Reparation

I took a seed with magical powers
To a region of the other world.
A mystical person had assured me
That certain events would then unfurl.

My brother was due for reincarnation
So I planted the seed in a healthy womb.
The blue-eyed boy was born again,
By the light of a waxing supermoon.

He flourished from the day of his birth
In the loving home of a family of four.
His happiness shone and he was free
Of the trauma that he had known before.

He married a girl of exquisite beauty
Who shared his adventures before
They had their two children and settled
In a haven on Anglesey's shore.

Sometimes, when the dawn was just breaking
He would go for a leisurely stroll,
Aware that a deep reparation
Was healing and cleansing his soul.

[11.07.20]

People Like Me

I will hear the sound of an overture,
Perhaps by Beethoven or Chopin,
When that glorious moment is at hand:
The blare of a trumpet to warn
Of imminent oblivion.

What then?
Indents of my feet in the sand
As I walk to that sacred land?
Angelic voices calling my name
As I try to exit once again?

No:
These romantic musings are futile
And scientific logic is the key:
When vital organs cease to function,
Life, and consciousness, cease to be.

Reaction:
Eager to go as soon as I can,
Without the trip to Switzerland.
Miracles are a rarity -
Beyond the grasp of people like me.

[11.07.20]

Succumb To Fantasy

Summer is slipping away,
Like an angel swiftly falling
From the edge of a precipice.
The thunderstorms are metaphors;
Driven by the deafening sound
Of a world afflicted by Lockdown.

Always something lurking to distort
The quest for paradise or rebirth:
Dreams splayed out on the seething pavement
Like flattened birds brought down in flight;
Happiness bound to dissipate
In the wilderness of the night.

The morning showers or rising sun
Proclaim the dawning of the day
In a non-disputable way:
But each is lost in a timeless
Psychological environ
That may succumb to fantasy.

[12.08.20]

Joy of Liberty

Dreams were tossed and hearts forlorn
In the last emotional storm.

Beauty has turned her face away
From the isolation and decay.

Images are jumbled and remain
Warped in a mind distorted with pain.

And my lonely soul is always longing
For the freedom death can bring.

Waiting for the soft rain on my skin,
The sense of peace to reign within.

Walking into that turbulent sea,
Knowing the joy of liberty.

[04.09.20]

No Advance and No Retreat

A swish of leaves on a September day
Evoked a sense of immediacy;
Time adrift and waiting to be filled,
Vast arenas of potential stilled.

Shadows take shape and vie for precedence
In a mind intent on recklessness.
The mirror image, hopeless to deny
Cruelty that alludes to days gone by:

Days gone by, played out in a parody
Of a present life marred by malady;
A set of repetitive entities
Violating with obscenities.

And the crucial question, not subdued,
Affronts the mind with great discord:
With no advance and no retreat
How can the past and future meet?

[06.09.20]

Ethereal Ally

Reading, writing, arithmetic,
Periodic tables and chemistry,
History, art and languages,
But – best of all – the poetry.

Childhood excursions outside of school;
Botanic gardens and galleries,
Rainy afternoons in libraries,
Absorbed in rhyming anthologies.

Adolescent angst and loss of sleep,
The pull of boys and film star vibes.
In the mesh of such confusion
Consult the wisdom of the scribes.

And again, when the heart has settled
On a love evoking joy and pain;
All of life and those shared moments
Captured in musings and refrains.

So much to follow: trips abroad,
Parties and rock concerts to attend,
Then trying to locate the self
In darkened rooms where words are penned.

University and lifelong friends,
A mind expanded and knowledge gained.
Romantic ties and the pace of life
Become impossible to sustain.

Cancer treatments and aftermath,
Protracted flirtation with death.
Inspiration re-emerges
To bind the soul to Mother Earth.

Loss of work and social status,
Lack of purpose and grave despair,
Flee from London to Anglesey
To seek an answer waiting there.

And all the while the rhyming haunts
Throughout the days and sleepless nights;
Ethereal ally to assist
The spirit in its earthly plight.

[09.09.20 – 11.09.20]

Bed of Sorrow

I'll meet you on Rainbow Bridge
As the Moon Turns The Tides.
I heard you call from Pali Gap
Where the Voodoo Chile abides.

I can't remain in this strange place
Or Wait Until Tomorrow.
I can Hear My Train A-Comin';
Raise me from my bed of sorrow.

[13.09.20]
Song titles by Jimi Hendrix

That Final Kiss

The bridge is shaky – precarious;
Wake up, Mary – it's hilarious!
Get the brush and sweep away
The debris from your own decay.

You can stroke my lifeless hand
When that moment is at hand.
There is still an essence that exists
When you impart that final kiss.

[14.09.20]

Heaven's Shore

He is the source of all beauty;
A light in every darkened place.
The subtle nuance of the soul
Is etched in his exquisite face.

He is the other part of me;
A dream wrapped in a rhapsody.
He gives me life when life is gone
And love to pin my hopes upon.

His gift to me on each new day
Is those blue eyes that can convey
The vast expanse that always seems
To bind our fate behind the scenes.

And so I'm bound to him until
I lose my courage and my will;
But we will meet where rainbows pour
Their rays of light on Heaven's shore.

[18.09.20 – To Gerry]

Those Violins

You are the tiny golden stars
That flow through every core of me
When my body is on the floor.
You are the warmth of a bright sun
And the sweet aroma
Of a budding sycamore.

Days of sorrow and regret,
And pain that propels a soul
Towards its ultimate goal,
Are freeze-framed when we move beyond
The screaming madness
Of the daily rigmarole.

And therein lies the secret
Of love and friendship
And anything of consequence.
In the end those violins
Regale us with the enigmatic sounds
Of comfort, peace and innocence.

[28.09.20]

Permanently Free

Pain

    Black

        Space

Death's

    Dark

        Face

Fire

    The

        Gun

Run

    Run

        Run

Need

    To

        Be

Permanently

        Free

[28.09.20]

Your Soul's Domain

On this day, first of October,
I saw an orange moon in the sky.
Seven hours prior to this,
Gerry Jones leaned across the table
And looked me squarely in the eye.

In equal measure these incidents
Served to take my breath away.
In equal measure they invoked
A sense of wonder I believed
Belonged to yesterday.

I thought the sun would never rise
And vengeful forces would disrupt
The motion of the rushing tide,
But sometimes light dispels the dark
And in your soul's domain resides.

[01.10.20]

Home

Let us tear off these bodies
And wander in the place
From which creativity stems.
Let us dance away from mortal life
And how it seeks to overwhelm.

You know we have already walked
In elevated realms
Where destiny has sung our song.
Her soft lament begins to soothe
As we hasten towards home.

Home is where we freely roam
Without the weight of human form
Or its superficial binds.
I find that it's discernible
When dreams command the waking mind.

[04.10.20]

Sullen Ghost

Devils in dark coats riding roughshod
Over my fragile hopes and dreams;
Cloven hooves pounding the dirt tracks
Where my heart lies in smithereens.

The midnight palpitations pound
Like stormy seas on ancient rocks,
Eroding visions of a girl
Adorned in medieval frocks.

Life slipping out of a body
That longs to settle in its tomb.
A sullen ghost regards the corpse
Recumbent in that lonely room.

[07.10.20]

Herculean Bond

They are motionless on the ground
While you are soaring to infinity.
I always knew that you were here -
Beyond, beside and within me.

They speak to me in gentle tones
Of trite conventionality.
You and I revoke the rules
And disregard the boundaries.

This makes me pour my aching soul
Into the vastness of your power.
This makes me give you all of me
In every fraught and pain-filled hour.

And, most of all, the way I love you,
Is not for this world to withstand.
There is a Herculean bond
That only we can understand.

[15.10.20 – to Gerry]

Christine

I once knew a psychic called Christine
Who lived in a pristine flat in Streatham.
She gave us Tarot lessons on a Monday night,
In the mystical glow of candlelight.

She had a ballerina's grace
And her youthful eyes could embrace
The most radical shift in the universe
Or the smallest menial request.

Christine wore a silver locket
Inscribed with the name of her thespian son.
It clinked on the top of the crystal ball
As the supernatural games begun.

The cards were laid out on a ruby cloth
And read by the group, with varying flair.
I was drawn by the charm of an artistic girl
With a quirky persona and bright auburn hair.

I then embarked on a path of meditation,
Marked by transcendental contemplation,
Led by Rajan Samra at his retreat -
A New Age shop on Streatham High Street.

Further studies and events -
Crystals, astrology and supplements,
Woven into a new philosophy
And placed in the book of poetry.

[18.10.20]

Love

Love is a strange thing -
Sometimes comforting,
At other times amusing
Or desperately confusing.

Love is so intense
And magnificent;
Utterly dependent
On its recipient:

Unconditional,
As in parental;
Or riding on the storm
Of the sibling bond;

Love of friends can be
Just like family;
And the true romantic state
Cannot be left to fate.

Love is exhilarating
And infuriating.
It teases with impulses
And readily repulses.

But, aside from all this,
Love equates with happiness.
Only love can save the soul
And reveal its Truth to all.

[19.10.20]

We Have Met Before

You know that we have met before,
In the shelter of an ancient glade.
When paradise unlocks its door,
The human embers start to fade.

In the shelter of an ancient glade,
I dance with you in beams of light.
The human embers start to fade,
The soul redeems its timeless flight.

I dance with you in beams of light,
Without restraint or backward glance.
The soul redeems its timeless flight,
Eternal in its permanence.

Without restraint or backward glance,
I'll give you all and everything.
Eternal in its permanence,
The joy that only love can bring.

I'll give you all and everything
When paradise unlocks its door.
With joy that only love can bring,
You'll know that we have met before.

[30.10.20]

The Ballerina

The marionettes are grinning
As they perch on the floral display.
The delicate china is rattling
As the tea slops onto the tray.

She carries it into the dark room
With the odour of musk and decay.
Each tick of the clock is a symbol
Of a life ebbing slowly away.

She can see a glimmer of sunlight
Through the gloom of the mist and the cloud;
A show-stopping ballerina
Propelled by the roar of the crowd.

The music builds to crescendo
And traverses the present and past.
The rigid restraints of her body
Courageously broken at last.

They said she looked calm and serene
When they found her laid out on the floor.
The music was still softly playing
But the clock was ticking no more.

[15.11.20]

Beyond The Mist

I thought I saw her through the mist
That settled on the snow-capped hill;
Dancing barefoot as a melody
Pierced the bitter Winter chill.

And then she sat most regally
In the comfort of her high-backed chair;
A playful smile upon her lips
And streaks of auburn in her hair.

I heard her laughter in the garden
Before the advent of the dawn.
The scent of jasmine permeated
Until her presence there was gone.

But she returned in silver moonlight,
A vision in a silken dress;
And later, in the dead of night,
I woke to feel her soft caress.

[25.11.20]

The Wildest of Unknown Places

I want to see that copper mountain
Or walk in corridors of ancient castles
Built by warring kings.
I want to run on sandy beaches
Where vast expanses of sea
Gently convey their history.

Another trip to Bull Bay or Red Wharf
Or the rugged terrain of the South Stack.
Take me back so that I can fill my lungs
With that pure Anglesey air
And feel one last surge of heroism
In my wilting form.

The piper is calling;
The roar is pounding in my head.
Place all your hopes in me
As I go intrepid into
The wildest of unknown places.

[25.11.20]

That's All

Free falling now;
One moment, not one day, at a time.
Keep the rhyme coming,
The guitar strumming,
The laughter and the wild Celtic man.
No need to reason or understand;
There is beauty in chaos -
No direction the best protection
From vanity and insanity.
Try for sleep, keep going
Till the final fall.
Turn out the light, that's all...

[25.11.20]

The Mystery

A dark speck in a vast space -
Member of the human race.
Head upturned to face the sun:
Anticipation of the one
Remarkable event or deed
That instigates a novel creed.

So the bibles are locked away
On the eve of the Pagan day.
The saints and sinners have now read
The Tibetan Book of the Dead;
Still the mystery is suppressed
Beneath the level of consciousness.

[22.12.20]

Blaze of Glory

Let's just be atoms and sit
In curious wonderment,
Without recourse to incessant chatter
Or the need to understand.

Let's open up our minds to lands
From which others have returned
With great rewards for humanity:

Darwin, Einstein, Watson and Crick,
Martin Luther King, The Dalai Lama;
Too many to mention in order
To underscore a point.

Let's aim for the highest tier
Of this all-too-short existence;
Make the best use of our
Evolutionary advantages

And go out in a Blaze of Glory!

[22.12.20]

Come To Life

Can I use my pain to gain
True insight into the human condition?

Am I hell-bent on chronicling
My dissent into madness
Or the space between it
And creativity?

I doubt the efficacy
Of such probing in the early hours,
When my powers are encumbered
By the ferocious need for sleep -

And yet it keeps
The literary wolf from the door.

The creeping sense of loneliness
Can be splurged on a page
Like the blood from a withdrawn dagger,
And I can stagger into the world of sleep
With a remote sense of achievement.

Hurry towards me in the dream world,
For that is the place
In which I truly come to life.

[22.12.20]

You Are Mine

Gerry Jones, a light shines
Through those soulful eyes
And transports me from
The dread of the mundane
To a much higher plane.

You can present in mortal form
Or reappear where angels meet
And kiss the rainbow beams
That stretch across a purer sky.

Your presence invokes the sense
That nothing is as it seems.
In the most sublime of moments
I capture you in my dreams;

The enigma unravelling like
A heart shattered from grief:
The breath slipping;
The earth wavering;
The unshakeable belief
That you are mine,

And then, PEACE!

[27.12.20]

Come Away With Me

Come away with me
To a shaded forest
Hidden from the world's view.
I want to dance with you;
Our dampened feet silken
In the soft leaves.

The rustle of the willow trees
Resets the rhythm
Of the wounded heart.
Persephone is waiting
To mobilise the ramparts:

No need for barriers
Where children sing
And float on elfin wings,
Where birds project their soothing song
To deities who simply long
For peace.

So, let us have that sweet release:
That rush of freedom
Echoed in the gushing waterfall.
Let me give you all
That I can ever be,
Come away and dance with me.

[26.03.21]

Short Stories and Factual Accounts

The Neighbour

Melissa – author

About a year ago my neighbour moved into the house opposite, which had been vacant since the previous owner died. The new lady, in her seventies, at a guess, seemed quiet and unassuming, and frequently pottered in her front garden. She seemed friendly with the young couple who lived next door, and she and I waved and called Hello whenever I stepped outside. Her son visited about once a week and she frequently had the builders in to complete renovations on the house. I decided to call her Mildred.

I though that Mildred's diary for a couple of days might read like this:

Day 1 – Monday 01 April 2019

I was up at 6:00 a.m. as usual, had breakfast and tidied up whilst waiting for the builders. I'm always glad to see them. Martin, the boss, is very nice and, well, it's a bit of company for me. They finished the bathroom on Friday and now they're going to make a start on the kitchen.

Martin and I always start with a cup of tea while the men are setting up, and he tells me exactly what they're going to do. I think he gets a bit frustrated with me because I keep forgetting to put my hearing aid in. Also, I forget things generally – that seems to be getting worse. I tried to pay him for the bathroom this morning but he said I had already paid him on Friday. I'm glad he's so honest!

It was noisy once the men started so I put on my old clothes and pottered in the garden for most of the afternoon. I saw the young woman across the road when she popped out to do the recycling. She seems to stay mainly at home.

Day 2 – Tuesday 02 April 2019

Martin and the lads needed to finish another job today so they will be back tomorrow. That means I had the day to myself. My son, David, called in for about an hour. He said Jane and the children are keeping well but work is stressful, as always. I'm very proud that he's a police officer but I do worry about him.

I spent most of the day cleaning and tidying and had a little nap when David left. After that I had a small meal – I don't eat much – then I relaxed in front of the TV and did some knitting. It'll be an early night for me.

Melissa – author

I hadn't been out properly for three years but it was my birthday and I was in need of a treat. It was just dinner with my best friend, Linda, but our time together is always special.

We were seated at the window of Linda's favourite restaurant, intermittently gazing at the stunning view of the Menai Straits, and sipping a lovely Sauvignon blanc as we engaged in our typically lively conversation. However, my concentration was broken by the arrival of a party of four new diners who were taken further along the restaurant. This party consisted of two elderly gentlemen, very well-dressed, a younger woman, perhaps in her fifties, and my neighbour, Mildred. She didn't notice me but I certainly noticed her because she was almost unrecognisable in comparison with her usual dowdy self.

Mildred was wearing a satin, emerald-coloured evening dress with tasteful court shoes and matching bag. She was fully made up and her demeanour was radically altered. She was poised, sophisticated and speaking very confidently and loudly. I couldn't help but glance at her throughout the evening, so struck was I by this unexpected encounter.

What struck me most about the group was the way in which Mildred and the two men fussed over the young woman in their company, who seemed considerably more subdued than her companions. I found the whole thing intriguing and, even more baffling, was the way in which everything returned to normal the following day. I saw Mildred pottering in her garden, in the usual unglamorous attire, and once again seeming as quiet and mousy as she had always been.

I was pondering the events of the night before as I was drinking my mid-morning tea and reading the local newspaper. My attention was immediately drawn to a bizarre headline and very strange report of the discovery of a woman's body in a woodland just a few miles from our village. The description perfectly fitted that of the woman I had seen with Mildred and her male friends the night before. The really upsetting part of the story was the news that the woman's body had been drained of blood and there were marks on her neck which appeared to have been made by an animal. Further investigations were proceeding.

Mildred's actual diary – Saturday 06 April 2019:

Last night was incredible. I never thought I would meet my own kind in a quiet village like this. And this aged, mortal body is a perfect cover for my ancient self. I can roam at night, unsuspected, and could even look for prey in the daytime, so harmless does my frail human self appear. That woman last night was certainly easily fooled, believing that we three could be even remotely interested in her silly little publishing business. It was easy to lure her to the woods with the promise of a nightcap and further discussions.

Her flesh was surprisingly tender for a woman in her fifties. It's a shame I couldn't share her with the men but I was starved of that essential fluid after all these years. We'll go out again soon so that they may feast.

I noticed the neighbour opposite in the restaurant, although she didn't realise that I had seen her. Best to keep a distance and yet keep her in my sights.

Marianne

'I told you we shouldn't have come. All I do is worry about her. And now we're in the middle of nowhere!'

'You've got to stop panicking. Your sister's gone AWOL before. And Leitrim's not the middle of nowhere. It's only a two-hour drive to Dublin.'

'She hasn't gone missing like this before. Mum has always found her reclusing in her flat, having one of her episodes. She's not there now and no-one has seen her for several days. I think I'll call the police.'

Michelle began to pace up and down the large sitting room of her husband's childhood home. His parents had moved to a more manageable bungalow just a mile away and Mark and his siblings now had the run of the old house as a holiday home.

'Come and sit down,' Mark said, a bit less sternly. 'Try to get some sleep and we'll check in with your parents again in the morning.'

"As if I'll be able to sleep!' Michelle cried. 'I didn't get a wink last night.'

'Well, at least get some rest.'

They settled down in the pitch dark at midnight and, despite her heavy fatigue, Michelle couldn't even close her eyes. Her mind was racing with thoughts of her sister, Marianne, who had always been prone to bouts of depression. One minute she was the life and soul, lighting up every room with her exuberant personality, and then she would crash and disappear for a few days, usually to self-medicate with alcohol in her tiny flat. After that, she would re-emerge and charm everyone with her presence again. But this was different; Michelle just knew it. She wanted to get up now and do something but the house was freezing so she just lay beside Mark and tried not to fidget too much.

Michelle awoke with a start and switched on her phone – 7:00 a.m. - she had been asleep for two hours. She jumped up, pulled on her heavy dressing gown and went to the bathroom. After a very quick wash, she went downstairs and put the kettle on. She would have a cup of tea then wake Mark and cook some breakfast.

An hour passed before Michelle pulled back the curtains in the sitting room and she was horrified by the sight that awaited her; a mountain of snow had accumulated overnight. The forecast had predicted it but not the deluge that had obviously occurred as they slept. She ran upstairs as quickly as she could and shook her husband awake.

'Mark, get up, we're snowed in!' she said frantically.

'What do you mean?'

'Snow – halfway up the house. What are we going to do?'

'We don't need to do anything, do we?' Mark said, yawning and rubbing the sleep from his eyes.

'Are you crazy! What if we need to go back to London, if something has happened to Marianne?' Michelle started pacing again.

'You're getting ahead of yourself. You need to calm down.'

Mark was out of bed now and he drew Michelle to him.

'Let's have breakfast and go from there. If we had to leave I could get Seamus to dig us out with the tractor. He's just a few miles down the road.'

They had breakfast and Mark built a fire then settled down to read. Michelle called her mother again on the landline, since the mobile signal was patchy to say the least.

'Still no news,' her mother said. 'I'll get your dad to call you as soon as we know anything, I promise.'

Michelle spent the day in a robotic-like state, completing chores and cooking lunch and dinner, just as she had done yesterday. She browsed through the silly magazines that she found in the drawer of the coffee table, and did whatever else she could to hide her frantic condition from Mark, who was now engrossed in his work on the laptop. So much for having a break from it all!

In the evening they watched a film and that night was a repeat of the previous two, with Mark fast asleep and Michelle staring into the darkness. When she did doze off, she must have slept for a bit longer because she awoke alone in bed, with the smell of bacon wafting up from the kitchen.

'You slept a bit better,' Mark said, setting down the bacon and scrambled eggs as Michelle seated herself at the kitchen table.

'Yes,' she said. 'Any news?'

'No, nothing, sorry! Eat your breakfast.'

This is ridiculous, Michelle thought. *I need to get home. I'll wait for a while and then start packing.* Once dressed, she sat in an old armchair by the fire in the snug, mesmerised by the sight of the falling snow outside. Mark was pottering about somewhere else in the house.

Suddenly, the phone rang in the hall and Michelle started from her reverie. She dashed out into the hall and grabbed the receiver. Mark was quickly at her side.

'Dad......,' she said.

Mark could hear her father's voice speaking in a low tone for a moment or two and then Michelle dropped the receiver onto the floor. Her face was ashen and he stepped forward to catch her before she fell.

The Irish Man

'That's not how you do a handstand!' the voice said as I toppled over once again.

My brother, Patrick, and I looked round and beheld the handsome brothers who had somehow come over the brow of the hill without our knowledge.

'This is how you do it!' Joe said as he not only perfected a handstand but walked a little way across the grass impressively aligned upside down.

'What do you think, Billy?' he called to his younger brother.

'That's the way to do it,' Billy said.

These brothers had become regular visitors to our flat in Maryhill, Glasgow. Patrick and I were completely in awe of them, not only because they were older, in their early twenties, but because of the way they dressed and their impeccable manners. Such gentlemen, they were!

Joe and Billy would sit on the rickety chairs in our filthy, run-down tenement flat, seemingly oblivious to the mess as they sat upright in their pristine suits and designer shoes. They drank from the dirty, chipped mugs, enquiring about the family's health, talking about sports and other topics with my father, and teasing me about boys that I might fancy. As if I would fancy boys when I was only twelve years old – the very idea!

Joe and Billy were friends with my cousin, Jason, who was living with us at the time, having had to flee from his brutal stepfather in

Ireland. The brothers visited us for months on end and then one day disappeared and never returned.

'Where are they?' I would ask Jason but he told me to be quiet. I kept asking, though, until Jason finally erupted, 'One's in hiding and the other is in prison.'

'I don't understand,' I said, wondering how such a fate could befall the charming men.

'They're bloody gangsters, you stupid girl!' Jason retorted, and no-one mentioned the brothers again.

I suppose it was useful to have known these shady characters early in my life, for various others were to follow. I encountered many of them in Glasgow's bedsit land, including a heroin addict, a cannabis-dealing Rastafarian and a beautiful Nigerian student who was almost continually stoned and surrounded by adoring women. Another memorable character was a large, dishevelled landlord with ten Alsatians in the basement and a wife who frequented the red light district to supplement their income.

My younger brother, John, and I, having shared these experiences, walked for miles every day, speaking of the better life that we craved.

A move to Dunbartonshhire did not lead to such an improvement in our precarious predicament. There, we unknowingly moved into a flat above which resided a dangerous gangster who had just been released from prison after a long stretch for attempted murder. Fortunately, he had a soft spot for me and nothing too untoward happened.

Following these events, there was much moving around, from Scotland to London and back, and eventually a permanent move to London. It was here that I met an extraordinary Irish man who changed my life forever. We developed a powerful romantic and spiritual bond, and he taught me how to love someone other than a sibling, and how to trust another human being and develop a sense of safety. Even when we parted, after almost fifteen years together, he continued to act as a key person in my life.

Twenty years on from my first encounter with the gangster brothers, at the age of thirty four, the girl from the slums was at university studying psychology. I could not say that it was smooth sailing from there since major traumas were to follow, including the death of my beloved John and my battle with cancer. However, by this time I had secured lifelong friendships at university and beyond, and I had learned to live a life enriched by love and trust. These gifts, bestowed by one special man, I will carry with me until the end of my days.

The White Palace

2002

After twenty years of painful, debilitating menses, I was sent to King's College Hospital, London, and informed that tests had revealed the presence of abnormal cells in the uterine cervix. These were proportedly removed by laser treatment under local anaesthetic which was nothing short of agonising.

2003

I was called once again to King's College Hospital and informed that the cellular changes were now severely abnormal and spreading rapidly. A biopsy under general anaesthetic was performed .

'We need to cut out the whole clump of cells,' the doctor had said at the pre-operative meeting.

'But, even if you do, is there a chance of further abnormalities?' I asked him.

'Yes, I'm afraid so.'

'OK, just remove my womb, I said. 'Then I would be safe, wouldn't I?'

'Well, yes, but I don't think we should do that.'

'Why not?'

'You're only thirty-three. You might want to have children.'

'No, I definitely won't ever have children,' I said resolutely.

'You might change your mind,' was the infuriating response.

'No, I won't change my mind. 'I'm certain about that!'

'We wouldn't perform a hysterectomy on someone of your age.'

'Fine,' I said, frustrated by the medic's stubborn position and patronising attitude.'

'I'll do it privately,' I said to my partner, Mike, when I had recovered from the surgery.

But I didn't and that was the crucial turning point in my life.

6th August 2007

After four years of continued and worsening symptoms, I was diagnosed with an aggressive form of cervical cancer. This diagnosis was delayed for six months after a routine smear test revealed the presence of the HPV virus. Despite my relaying great concern to the GP informing of this, I was told, 'Let's just wait for six months and see what happens.'

What happened? During this six-month period, the cancer had a chance to spread from the cervix into the blood vessels outside. Consequently, the full course of aggressive treatment was required: five weeks of radiotherapy, with treatment every weekday and weekends to rest; chemotherapy once a week; and an horrific sixteen-hour session of brachytherapy – during that particular trauma I telephoned Mike from my hospital bed and told him, 'This is going to destroy me, or possibly even kill me.'

I never recovered. Fourteen years of unmanageable ill-health followed and my life as I knew it slipped away from me, bit by bit, gruelling year after gruelling year, until there was nothing left.

But now I am happy. I live in a white palace in the land which the living can only frequent in dreams. I wander out every vibrant day and walk without hindrance or care to an oak tree by a stream, and there I sit with my beloved brother, John, as the birds twitter and butterflies dance around us. Each moment is a glorious eternity of peace, joy and contentment. I have learned to pass through the veil and I go to my loved ones during their most serene moments and when they are in distress. I can also, easily, slip through the portal of dreams and engage with those special ones. Sometimes we just talk but at other times we walk in the sunshine or the rain, and they can feel my presence more acutely than that of the living people around them.

There is tremendous fun to be had in and beyond this sacred place. One of my highlights was an acoustic rendition of 'Hear My Train A Comin' by the wonderful Jimi Hendrix, just for me. That is Heaven indeed!

When the time comes, I will be delighted to meet you in this better world.

The Piano Room

My piano room, situated at the top of the stairs, is blessed with a glorious sea view. The furniture therein consists solely of the piano, one bookshelf and a comfortable chair placed in front of the window, in the prime position to admire the view.

This is my sanctuary. I come here straight after breakfast in the morning for a half-hour session on the piano and return in the evening to read my latest book. Following either of these activities I sit in the chair, gaze at the great expanse of water and remove myself from all maladies and concerns.

Today was particularly therapeutic – perhaps best described in poetic form:

Here I sit in the dreamy throes
Of a multitude of joys and sins,
Racing down long corridors to find
A place of ancient worshipping.

I open up the first door and see
An infant's mother with auburn hair,
Then business men in pristine suits,
Their worn-out faces lined with care.

I move on down the corridor
And find a wide array of things;
Elfin dancing in fairy rings,
And maidens serving portly kings.

Further on, down winding steps,

A thousand candles burning bright;
A new door opens and I am bathed
In the warming glow of a hallowed light.

But finally I find my home
Behind the door where the spirits roam,
Where the music plays and starts to soothe
The lonely heart and the sullen muse.

I awake from my reverie, open my eyes and gaze
upon the beauty of the Irish sea. A new sense of
calm has descended and I have the sense that I
am not alone. I dismiss it and go for my regular
stroll. The world looks different, brighter, as
though illumined by some indeterminate source.

     I return home, perform my usual tasks
and return to the piano room for my evening
reading session. There is a great expansion of
space and I feel that I have permanently
infiltrated a beauteous, magical realm.